How
your body
works

What happens
when your
heart beats?

Jacqui Bailey

WAYLAND

First published in 2007
by Wayland

Copyright © Wayland 2007

Wayland
338 Euston Road
London NW1 3BH

Wayland Australia
Level 17/207 Kent Street
Sydney NSW 2000

Senior Editor: Jennifer Schofield
Consultant: Dr Patricia Macnair
Designer: Phipps Design
Illustrator: Ian Thompson
Picture Researcher: Kathy Lockley
Proofreader: Susie Brooks

Picture acknowledgements
Walt Disney Pictures/The Kobal Collection/Richard Cartwright: 11; Tony
Freeman/Art Directors Photo Library: Cover, 26; Kolvenbach/Alamy Images: 27
London Aerial Photo Library/Corbis: 20; Medical-on-Line/Alamy Images: 25
Susumu Nishinaga/Science Photo Library: 18; Helene Rogers/Art Directors
Photo Library: 23; Mark Seelen/zefa/Corbis: 6; Manfred Vollmer/Still Pictures: 24
Ben Walsh/zefa/Corbis: 15T; Henry Westheim Photography/Alamy Images: 13
Watts/Wayland Archive: 8, 12, 15B, 22

CIP Data
 Bailey, Jacqui
  What happens when our heart beats? - (How does your body work?)
  1. Cardiovascular system - Juvenile literature
  I. Title
  612.1

ISBN: 978 0 7502 5128 0

Printed in China

Wayland is a division of Hachette Children's Books

Contents

Why does your heart beat?

Your heart beats to pump blood around your body. Blood is the red, sticky liquid that oozes out of your skin when you cut yourself.

Blood flows from your heart, around your body and back to your heart again. It is carried inside thousands of narrow tubes called blood vessels. Blood vessels reach into every part of your body. The flow of blood around your body is called the bloodstream.

Each time your heart beats, blood is pushed out of the heart and into the blood vessels. This forces the blood already in the blood vessels to move along. The next time your heart beats, the blood is moved on again – and again, around and around your body.

An adult's body has about five litres of blood in it. Your body has less – about two or three litres.

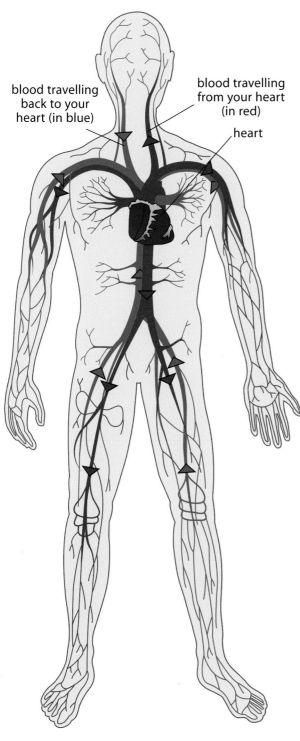

blood travelling back to your heart (in blue)

blood travelling from your heart (in red)

heart

Here you can see the main blood vessels in your circulation system. Blood vessels carry blood away from your heart, around your body and back to your heart again.

Your heart never stops beating, so your blood never stops moving. If it did you would be dead. This non-stop movement of blood around your body is called your circulation. It takes your heart less than a minute to pump all your blood three times around your whole body.

See for yourself

Pumping blood

Fill an empty squeezy bottle with water. Point the bottle into the bath or onto the garden. Squeeze it hard in the middle and water will shoot out of the tip. Your hand is pumping the water out of the bottle in much the same way as your heart pumps blood into your blood vessels.

What is blood for?

Your body is built from millions of tiny bits called cells. Cells need oxygen, food and water to keep them alive and healthy. Your blood brings all these things to your cells.

Oxygen is in the air that you breathe into your lungs. It passes from your lungs into your blood vessels and is carried along in your blood. Food is broken up into tiny pieces in your stomach. Below your stomach is a long, folded-up tube called the intestines. The broken-up food moves from your stomach into the intestines, and then the useful bits pass into your bloodstream, along with water from the food or from drinks.

As the blood travels around your body, the oxygen, food and water are taken out by your cells and used to release energy. Your body uses energy all the time, to live and grow.

Your blood is your body's postal service. It carries vital materials around your body and delivers them to your cells.

Energy lets you do all the things that you want your body to do. When the cells release energy they also produce waste. Your blood collects the waste and removes it.

Your blood does other jobs, too. It helps your body to heal itself and to fight off germs and diseases. It also spreads warmth from the centre of your body right to the ends of your fingers and toes.

Eating iron

The red cells in your blood need iron to keep them healthy. Foods such as eggs, red meat and dark green vegetables contain iron. Eating these foods regularly helps to keep up the levels of iron in your blood.

Your blood is made of cells, too. There are three main types: red blood cells, white blood cells and platelets. They float in a watery liquid called plasma.

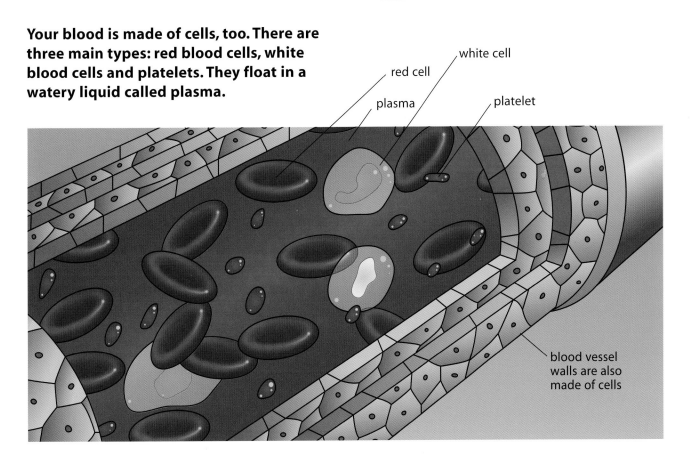

red cell

white cell

plasma

platelet

blood vessel walls are also made of cells

How big is your heart?

Make a fist. Your heart is much the same size as your fist, but it has hollow spaces inside it. When you are an adult, your heart will weigh about 200–300 grammes – that is as much as two apples.

Your heart is in the middle of your chest, inside your rib cage. The bottom of your heart tilts a little towards the left.

Your ribs form a bony cage that helps to protect your heart.

heart

ribs

Put the fingers of your left hand just below the curve of your left ribs. Can you feel something beating? That is your heart.

Sometimes your heart beats a bit faster, and sometimes a little slower. Generally, an adult's heart beats about 70 times a minute – just faster than once every second. In a year your heart will beat more than 36 million times.

Long ago, people used to believe that feelings of happiness or sadness came from the heart. This may be because our hearts beat faster when we get excited or scared. Now we know that feelings come from the brain, and our brain tells the heart how fast to beat. But we still often use the heart as a symbol for love and for bravery.

The biggest heart

The blue whale is the biggest animal in the world, and it has an equally big heart. Its heart is the same size as a Volkswagen Beetle car!

We draw pictures in the shape of a heart when we want to say that we love someone. Our actual heart does not really look like this!

Finding your pulse

Every time your heart beats and pushes blood into your blood vessels, a wave rolls through your bloodstream. The wave makes your blood vessels throb. This is called your pulse.

There are places on your body where you can feel your pulse. One of the best places is on the inside of your wrist, just below your thumb. Slide your fingers around your wrist until you feel a small beat just under the skin. This is your pulse.

Find a watch or clock that shows the seconds. Sit quietly while you count how many beats happen in 15 seconds. If you multiply the number of beats by four, you will know how many times your heart beats in one minute.

You can feel your pulse on the inside of your wrist. Lightly press the tips of two fingers on the outer edge of your wrist.

12

Jump up and down on the spot for a few minutes and then count the number of beats again. You should find that your heart beats more quickly when you move about – and the faster you move, the faster your heart beats. This is because your body is working harder and using more energy, so your heart has to work harder, too. It has to bring your cells more food and oxygen to give you the extra energy your body needs.

Fast and slow

Small animals usually have a faster heartbeat than larger ones. A mouse's heart beats 500 times in one minute. An elephant's heart beats about 35 times a minute. Usually a child's heartbeat is faster than an adult's.

Made of muscle

Your heart is made of muscle. You have lots of muscles in your body, and they all do the same thing – they give your body movement.

All muscles work in the same way. They contract, or tighten, and get shorter, or they relax and get longer. Some muscles contract and pull on your bones to move parts of your body, such as your arms and legs. Other muscles move things around inside you. Your stomach muscles contract and relax to break up the food in your stomach, for example. Your heart muscles contract and relax to move your blood.

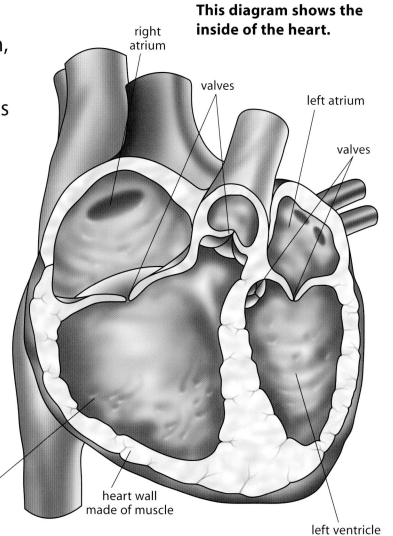

This diagram shows the inside of the heart.

right atrium

valves

left atrium

valves

right ventricle

heart wall made of muscle

left ventricle

You can make your arm and leg muscles work whenever you want them to, but your heart and stomach muscles work automatically – you cannot make them stop or start.

The inside of your heart is divided into two sides. If you think of your heart like a tiny house, each side has an upper room or chamber, called the atrium, and a lower chamber called the ventricle. Flaps, called valves, separate the atria (atria is the plural of atrium) from the ventricles . The valves open and close like doors to let blood flow from the top chambers to the bottom ones.

Your leg and arm muscles tire out when you use them a lot, and they need resting. Your heart never rests – it just keeps beating all the time.

See for yourself

Hard squeeze

Hold a tennis ball in one hand and squeeze it hard. This is how hard your heart muscle works to pump blood. How many times can you squeeze the tennis ball before you have to stop for a rest? Your heart never stops.

Heart at work

When your heart beats and the muscles in your heart contract, they squeeze all the blood out of your heart. When your heart muscles relax, more blood rushes in.

Blood flows into both sides of your heart at the same time. The left side fills up with blood from your lungs. This blood is full of oxygen. The right side fills up with blood from your body. This blood has very little oxygen as most of it has been used by your cells.

The blood fills the upper chambers, the atria, first.

See for yourself

Double beat

Try putting your ear close to a friend's chest to hear their heartbeat. If you listen very carefully you may be able to hear that each heartbeat makes two sounds – DE-DUM. The sounds are made by the two sets of valves closing, first between the atria and ventricles, then between the ventricles and blood vessels.

Then the muscles in the atria contract, pushing the blood through the valves into the the ventricles. This is the first half of your heart action.

Almost immediately, the valves shut to stop the blood flowing back into the atria and the muscles in your ventricles contract. This is the second half of your heartbeat. It is much stronger than the first.

The valves at the top of the ventricles are pushed open. The oxygen-rich blood in your left ventricle floods into the blood vessel leading to the rest of your body. At the same time, the oxygen-poor blood in your right ventricle goes into a blood vessel that leads to your lungs. The valves to your blood vessels snap shut and your heart relaxes.

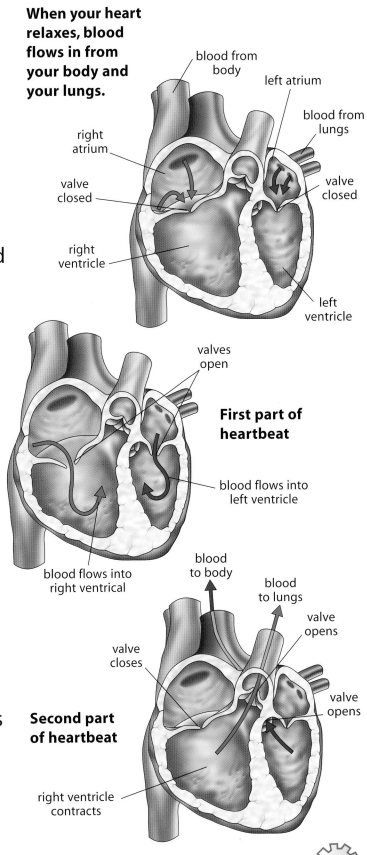

When your heart relaxes, blood flows in from your body and your lungs.

blood from body

left atrium

right atrium

blood from lungs

valve closed

valve closed

right ventricle

left ventricle

valves open

First part of heartbeat

blood flows into left ventricle

blood flows into right ventrical

blood to body

blood to lungs

valve opens

valve closes

valve opens

Second part of heartbeat

right ventricle contracts

Around and around

The blood that leaves the left side of your heart sets off on a journey to every part of your body. This journey takes about 20 seconds.

The blood vessels carrying the oxygen-rich blood from your heart are called arteries. The artery leading from your heart is the largest in your body. It is about as thick as your thumb. It divides into smaller and smaller arteries that branch out through your body like the roots of a plant.

Leading away from the smallest arteries are billions of even smaller tubes called capillaries. Capillaries are narrower than the hairs on your head and they spread out to reach all the other cells in your body. The walls of the capillaries are so thin that oxygen and the plasma in blood are able to pass through them into the cells on the other side.

Blood travels from the heart to the rest of the body through a network of arteries and capillaries.

capillaries   artery

18

The capillaries are so narrow that only a few red blood cells can move along them at the same time.

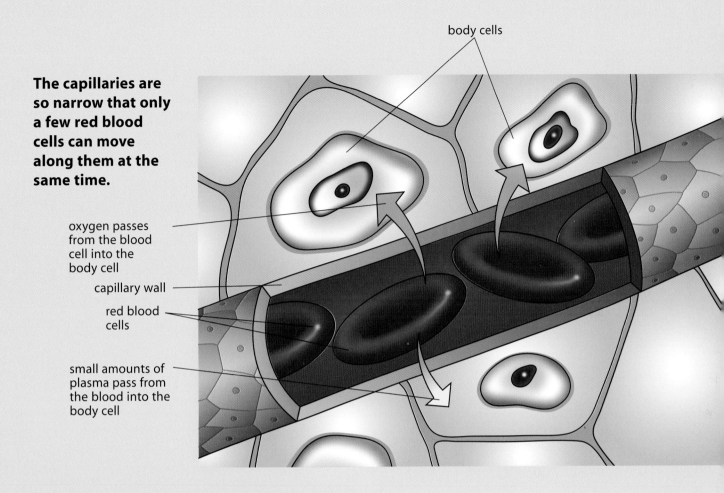

body cells

oxygen passes from the blood cell into the body cell

capillary wall

red blood cells

small amounts of plasma pass from the blood into the body cell

Oxygen is carried in your blood by the red blood cells. It is the oxygen in these cells that gives blood its bright red colour. As the red blood cells travel along the capillaries, oxygen moves from them into the body cells. Plasma carries tiny specks of food as well as water. As plasma passes into the body cells, it takes the food with it.

New blood for old

Blood cells are continually wearing out and have to be replaced. Some last just a few days and others a few months. Your body makes new blood cells all the time. Most are made in the jelly-like stuff called bone marrow that runs through the middle of your bones.

19

Back again

As oxygen, food and water pass into your cells, waste material passes out of them and into your blood.

Most of the waste material is the gas carbon dioxide. Some of the carbon dioxide is picked up by red blood cells, but most of it is carried in the plasma, along with other waste, such as unwanted food and water.

Blood carrying waste flows from the capillaries into a second set of blood vessels called veins. These lead back to the heart. On the way, the blood passes through the liver and the kidneys where some of the waste is taken out. This waste becomes part of the liquid that leaves your body when you wee.

Veins and arteries are like the two separate sides of a motorway – with each side going in a different direction. They meet only at the capillaries.

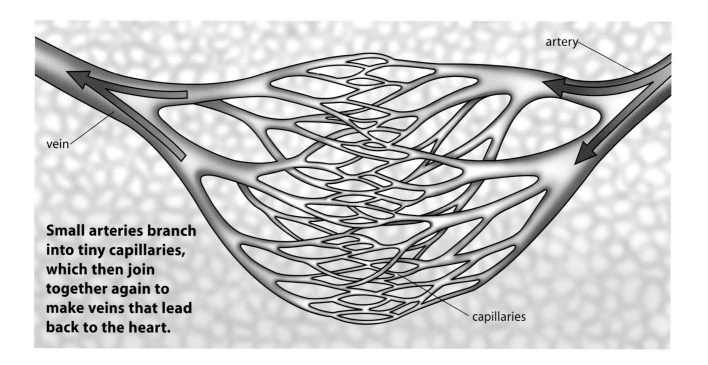

artery

vein

Small arteries branch into tiny capillaries, which then join together again to make veins that lead back to the heart.

capillaries

Finally, the blood reaches the two largest veins, which empty into the right side of the heart. From here the blood is pumped to the lungs. This is where carbon dioxide leaves the blood and more oxygen is picked up.

The carbon dioxide leaves our lungs when we breathe out. The oxygen-rich blood returns to the left side of the heart and is sent off on its journey again.

See for yourself

Blue blood

Veins lie closer to the skin than arteries. You can see them on the inside of your wrists as faint blue lines. Blood with lots of oxygen is bright red, but as the oxygen is taken out the blood becomes darker. The blood in veins is dark red, but your skin makes your veins look blue.

Blood battles

The other really important thing your blood does is help your body to fight off germs that could make you ill.

We are surrounded by really tiny living things called bacteria and viruses. Some bacteria are good for us, but many are not. Those that can harm us are known as germs. Whenever germs get into your body, the white blood cells in your blood do their best to hunt them down and destroy them.

If you cut yourself, germs can get inside the cut and cause an infection. You also lose blood from a cut.

Washing up

Whenever you put food or your fingers into your mouth, you could be putting germs into your body. The best way to protect yourself from germs is to wash your hands regularly with soap and water, especially before handling food.

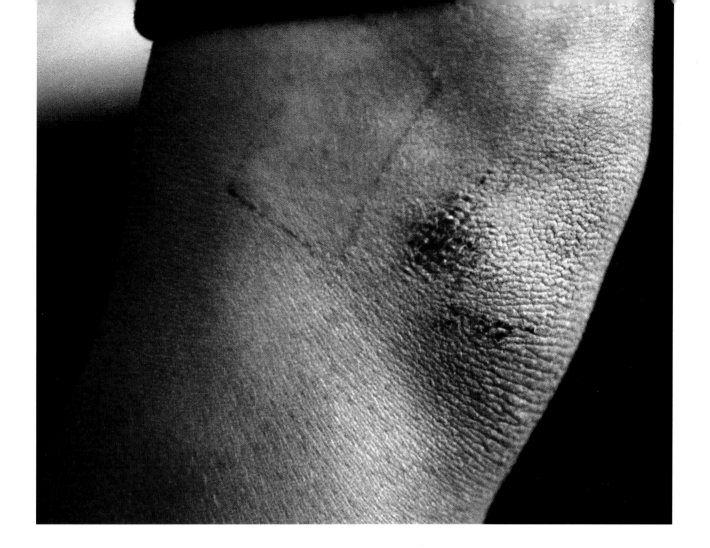

If you did not stop a cut from bleeding you could eventually bleed to death. Blood has the answer though. White blood cells and the tiny cells called platelets gather around the cut. The white blood cells fight off any germs, while the platelets stick together to make a plug known as a scab.

The scab dries out and forms a protective cover over the wound until the skin has a chance to grow back. When the cut is completely healed the scab falls off, sometimes leaving a scar.

A scab is like a natural plaster. It stops blood from leaking out of a wound and stops germs from getting into the wound.

Giving blood

When people lose a lot of blood through a bad accident or an operation, their body cannot replace the blood quickly enough. Often, they have to be given another person's blood.

When someone is given blood it is called a blood transfusion. A doctor puts a hollow needle with a tube attached to it into one of the patient's veins. At the other end of the tube is a bag of blood. The blood drips down the tube, through the needle and into the patient.

People who give blood usually give about half a litre at a time. It is not too painful to give blood and your body soon makes more blood to replace it.

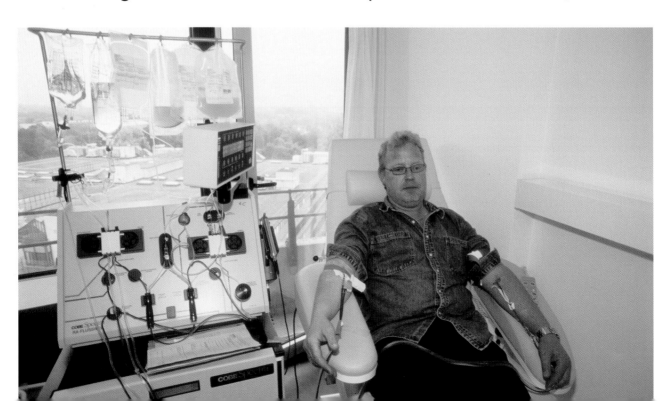

Before having a blood transfusion, the patient's own blood is tested to find out which blood group he or she belongs to. The blood given in a transfusion must be the same type, or the person will become ill.

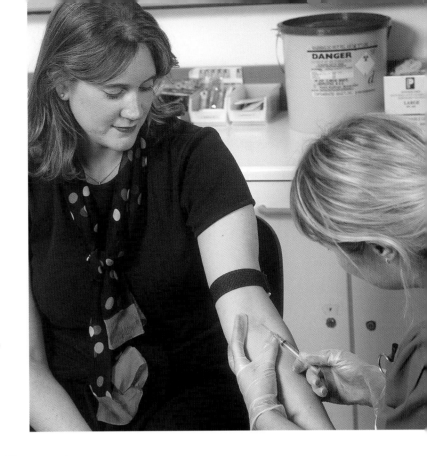

The blood used in blood transfusions comes from people called blood donors. Any healthy adult can be a blood donor. The blood is collected from one of the donor's veins through a needle and a tube, but this time the blood runs out of the body and into a bag. The bag is stored in a hospital refrigerator until it is needed. Hospitals need supplies of healthy blood all the time to treat people who are injured or ill. It is very important that healthy adults give blood when they can.

We do not all have exactly the same blood. There are four main blood types, called Group A, Group B, Group AB and Group O. Most people have Group O blood.

Drain away

Hundreds of years ago, doctors thought that if they drained some blood from people who were ill they would let out the sickness along with the blood. Unfortunately, this did not work, it just made the sick person weaker.

Healthy heart

Your heart is the most hard-working muscle in your body. But it can easily become damaged over time.

Like any muscle, your heart has to be exercised regularly to keep it strong and healthy. When you run or play sports you can usually feel your heart pumping faster and harder. It is good for your heart to do this as it helps to keep it working properly throughout your life.

The more you exercise your lungs and heart, the healthier they are. Cycling, swimming and running are all good ways to exercise.

If people eat a lot of rich and fatty foods, too much fat builds up in their blood. The fat may form a layer on the inside of blood vessels, making them narrower and even blocking them. When this happens, blood cannot move easily around your body and oxygen cannot get to your cells. If the heart cannot get enough oxygen, some of the heart muscle will die. This is called a heart attack. If parts of your brain are starved of oxygen, brain cells will die and your brain may not work properly. This is called a stroke.

Smoking and drinking too much alcohol are also harmful to your heart. The best way to look after your heart is to exercise regularly, eat a healthy diet with lots of fruit, vegetables, grains and beans – and do not smoke.

Doctors say that we should eat at least five pieces or helpings of fresh fruit or vegetables every day.

Water supply

Your body uses up about two litres of water every day washing out the waste materials that collect in your blood. That water needs to be replaced. The best way to do this is to drink two litres (about eight glasses) of plain water every day.

Body words

Words shown in italics, *like this*, are a guide to how a particular word sounds.

Arteries
Blood vessels that carry blood away from the heart.

Atria *(ay-tree-uh)*
The two hollow upper chambers inside the heart. One atria is called an atrium.

Blood donor
Someone who gives some of his or her blood to be used by other people who are ill or who have lost a lot of blood.

Blood transfusion
Putting blood into people who have lost a lot of their own blood, or replacing someone's unhealthy blood with new, healthy blood.

Blood vessels
The network of tubes that carry blood to every part of your body. Blood vessels include arteries, veins and capillaries.

Capillaries *(ca- pil-la-reez)*
The smallest blood vessels in the body. They link the arteries to the veins.

Cells
Tiny bits of living material from which all of the parts of your body are built. There are lots of different types of cells in your body, for example red blood cells and white blood cells. Most single cells are too small to be seen without a microscope.

Circulation
The flow of blood from your heart, through the blood vessels and back to your heart again.

Plasma
The liquid part of blood that carries all the blood cells, food and other chemicals around your body.

Platelets
Small cell flakes that float in your blood and help to plug cuts.

Pulse
The throb in your blood vessels caused by blood being pumped from your heart. Counting your pulse tells you how fast your heart is beating.

Red blood cells

The cells in your blood that carry oxygen and give blood its red colour. There are hundreds more red cells in your blood than white cells.

Valves

The flaps in your heart that stop blood from flowing backwards.

Veins

Blood vessels that carry blood back to the heart after the oxygen has been taken out of it by your body cells.

Ventricles

The two hollow lower chambers inside the heart.

White blood cells

The cells in your blood that search out and destroy germs. White cells are much larger than red cells, but there are fewer of them.

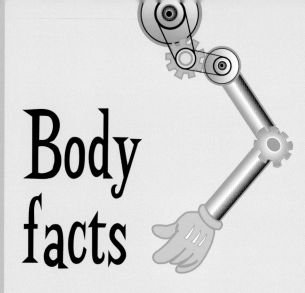

Body facts

- If all your blood vessels were joined together they would reach more than twice around the world.

- The walls of a capillary are only one cell thick.

- Plasma makes up more than half of your blood.

- Red blood cells last for about four months.

- Your body makes about three million red blood cells every second, and just as many die every second.

- You have anything from 100 to 10,000 bacteria on each square centimetre of your skin – most of them harmless.

Index